I'LL EAT YOU LAST:
A CHAT WITH SUE MENGERS

I'LL EAT YOU LAST:
A CHAT WITH SUE MENGERS

a new play by
JOHN LOGAN

OBERON BOOKS
LONDON

WWW.OBERONBOOKS.COM

First published in 2013 by Oberon Books Ltd
521 Caledonian Road, London N7 9RH
Tel: +44 (0) 20 7607 3637 / Fax: +44 (0) 20 7607 3629
e-mail: info@oberonbooks.com
www.oberonbooks.com

A catalogue record for this book is available from the British Library.

PB ISBN: 978-1-84943-414-0
E ISBN: 978-1-84943-938-1

Cover photography by Ellen von Unwerth

Printed, bound and converted
by CPI Group (UK) Ltd, Croydon, CR0 4YY.

Visit www.oberonbooks.com to read more about all our books
and to buy them. You will also find features, author interviews and
news of any author events, and you can sign up for e-newsletters
so that you're always first to hear about our new releases.

<u>WARNING</u>

This play contains profanity, smoking, alcohol consumption, drug use, and gossip.

CHARACTERS
SUE MENGERS

SETTING
The living room of Sue Mengers' Beverly Hills home...1981.

This play should be performed without an intermission.

I'll Eat You Last: A Chat With Sue Mengers was first performed at the Booth Theatre, New York on April 5, 2013 with the following cast and creative team:

<u>*Cast*</u>

SUE MENGERS — Bette Midler

<u>*Creative Team*</u>

Playwright	John Logan
Director	Joe Mantello
Scenic Designer	Scott Pask
Costume Designer	Ann Roth
Lighting Designer	Hugh Vanstone
Sound Designer	Fitz Patton
Associate Director	William Joseph Barnes
Production Manager	Juniper Street Productions, Inc.
Props	Kathy Fabian
Stage Manager	Laurie Goldfeder
General Manager	101 Productions, Ltd.
Producers	Graydon Carter
	Arielle Tepper Madover
	James L. Nederlander
	The Shubert Organization
	Terry Allen Kramer
	Stephanie P. McClelland
	Jeffrey Finn
	Ruth Hendel
	Larry Magid
	Jon B. Platt
	Scott and Brian Zeilinger

Dedicated to Brian Siberell and James Bagley

Who I believe would eat me almost last.

Curtain up to reveal...

The living room of Sue Mengers' Beverly Hills house... Pale colors, pale flowers... Tasteful and designed.

SUE MENGERS relaxes comfortably on her luxurious sofa. She wears one of her signature caftans and wire-rim glasses. There's a coffee table before her with a dish of chocolates, an ashtray, and some objects d'art.

She smokes, constantly.

She looks at the audience, a gaze at once baleful and mischievous. And always there's the wicked sparkle.

SUE: I'm not getting up... It's my house, you get up. Only don't. I just had the carpet cleaned for the party. Don't take offense but the carpet is for the guests tonight. You will be long gone by then. Oh yes, long gone and back to Van Nuys or wherever you hail from, by way of too many freeways I'm sure, poor lambs, I'm weeping for you already. Honestly, you see that tear?

So forgive me for not getting up. Imagine me as that caterpillar from *Alice in Wonderland*, the one with the hash pipe. He didn't need to get up. He could sit there and look over his domain and torment that little brat. He was a smartass for sure, but he had some brio. Lemme tell you, all that worm needed was a three-line phone and he could have been the best agent in Wonderland... Yes, you notice the phone.

There's a phone on the table next to her.

Now it's not my normal practice to have a phone in the living room. I think it's rude to be in the middle of some <u>fascinating</u> conversation with a starlet about which plum role she's trying to get – meaning which director she's trying to screw to land said plum – and all of a sudden the phone rings and before you know it you're embroiled with the travails of a client. Movie stars never have problems; they only have <u>travails</u>… So the phone is usually banished to other parts of the house. But tonight I'm expecting an important call… Yes, you all know, The Call.

We might as well talk about the elephant in the room.

A glance to the audience: I dare you.

I'm on the edge of my seat, metaphorically speaking, for the call that will bring the dulcet tones of Ms. Streisand to my ears. It will come when it will come, Barbra-time being elastic and elliptical. I'll let it ring twice or even three times if I'm feeling cheeky and then we'll <u>dish</u>. I love a dish with Barbra. She who came up with me. She who is my good right arm. She who is me if I'd had any talent. She of the nails and the voice and now the perm, which we will <u>not</u> discuss. She who fired me today.

No, to be accurate, her lawyers fired me. Her microstate of serious Jews that joined arms and bottle-danced their way to the speaker-phone and pressed my button… Speaker-phone, what a

villainous invention. All the intimacy of a proper
phone call gone. All the purring seduction of setting
the phone on the pillow next to you replaced by
"What? Who said that? Which kike am I talking
to?" ... I had one of those new car phones installed
once. Size of a dismembered baby's torso. Well, I
tried using it but it took all the fun out of driving
around trying to run over Faye Dunaway...

So the firm of Mandelbaum, Schwartz, Speer and
Goebbels promised me Barbra would call me
herself tonight. I wait. All on pins and needles.
Can't you tell?

*She grandly brushes her hair back, a signature gesture,
very Veronica Lake.*

You like the place? My modest little hacienda in the
Hills of Beverly. Previously owned by Miss Zsa Zsa
Gabor, a star of the highest magnitude. For weeks
after moving in I was finding little bits of marabou
and sequins. Everywhere you looked: marabou
and sequins. Like she shit them. So after having the
house fully de-sequined I had my queens come in
to decorate. Tip from Sue: if you're not particularly
domestic yourself, as I am not, you want the place
shrieking with queens. Don't get in the way, let
them flutter.

Actually I did have one argument with my
decorating boys. They insisted on putting in the
pool. You cannot have, they averred, a Beverly Hills

mansion without a pool. You will lose the respect
of your friends and neighbors. You will lose tiles in
the great Mah Jong game that is Hollywood. So I let
them put in the fucking pool... *(She gestures vaguely
behind her.)* ... It's out there somewhere. I'm not
really sure. "Exercise" doesn't play a big part in my
life. By this time your Sue has embraced her inner
zaftig.

She laughs; a low, wicked, delightful sound.

*Then she takes a chocolate from the little dish on the
coffee table before her. Eats it. Yum.*

Besides, my husband loves a little jiggle. Ah, yes,
my beloved spouse. Jean-Claude Tramont's his
name, Belgian, yum. He's what we call a hyphenate:
writer-director-producer. Generally in Hollywood
the more titles you attach to your name the less
successful you are. But fair enough, he's in the
game like everyone else. We're one of those typical
Hollywood couples: on a good night we're Nick and
Nora Charles; on a bad night we're Nick and Nora
Charles Manson.

But I love him to little tiny pieces. And the only
thing I love more than my husband is my <u>dinner
parties</u>. Is there anything more sublime than hosting
twelve of your nearest and dearest for an evening
of good chat? That's what we do here: <u>we</u> <u>dish</u>.
Who's in, who's out, who's up, who's down, who's
on bottom, who's on top but really wants to be

on bottom. It's the most delicious gossip you ever heard. I love gossip, don't you? 'Tis like mother's milk to me, and it's the lube by which this town slips it in. Whole place would grind to a slow, agonizing dry hump without gossip… Like I always say: if you can't say anything nice about someone, come sit by me.

She laughs.

Okay, that wasn't me. That was Alice Longworth. Or Halston. Who remembers? It doesn't matter. You hear a good story you claim it like a conquistador planting the flag, honey. Most of the stories I hear about myself are sheer fantasy, as are most of the stories I tell about myself. But why use your own boring stories when stealing your friends' is so much more fun? And in Hollywood there's no such thing as stealing anyway. Oh no, not at all. When Brian DePalma rips off Hitchcock it's not theft – it's homage. We pay a fuck of a lot of homage out here.

For all you simple homemakers out there, like me, here's the big secret to a successful dinner party: only invite movie stars. They won't come, but you'll have made the effort.

You cannot imagine the pleasure I get casting the parties: looking out over the glittering landscape of Hollywoodland and Broadwayville, seeing who's out of rehab and might need a drink, checking on

15

the latest star signed with another agent I need
to steal... Only thing is, all my guests have to be
<u>famous</u>. Honey, my own mother couldn't get in
if she were standing outside in the rain... It's all
Twinklies here! I love my stars! I love 'em! So when
I'm planning a party I go into conclave and give it
a good old think, then I send out the white smoke
and the invitations are issued hither and yon. But
Sue has to be careful because...<u>it's all business</u>.
Everything in this town is business. We're a
company town and anyone who tells you otherwise
is misinformed.

Right in there, at my table, deals are brokered;
careers come to life or die untimely deaths.
There's not a dinner I give where I'm not trying
to get a client a job. It's one long audition. I seat
the delightfully hyphenated Ann-Margret next to
divinely talented Mike Nichols and she's in *Carnal
Knowledge* by dessert. Burt Reynolds shares a beer
with Alan Pakula and he's landed *Starting Over*.
Lauren Hutton meets Paul Schrader and walks away
with *American Gigolo*. I love it! I love my job!

But I really only have two hard and fast rules about
throwing parties, which you are encouraged to
employ:

Rule Number One: All showbiz all the time. Don't
talk to me about politics, science, sports, or animal
husbandry, I don't give a shit. The only thing I
care about is movies and movie stars. Nothing

will make me snooze faster then some goddamn celebrity opining on matters global. Honestly, Henry Kissinger is only interesting to me because he's fucking Jill St. John. ... Now back in what we dinosaurs refer to as "the sixties" everyone had to get deeply political. Suddenly all the stars were wearing headbands and getting awfully earnest about Attica or Kent State or Cambodia. Is there anything more boring than Cambodia? No one shoots a movie there. No one vacations there. Can I find it on a map? Do I own a map? What the fuck are these people talking about?! ... *(Pretends to fall asleep.)* ... Zzzzz. ... I just don't understand why anyone would talk about anything other than show business. I don't care what it is. Vanessa Redgrave comes over once and she's sitting there, downing glass after glass of my best Veuve Clicquot like a good Socialist, chattering on about Palestine or the grape boycott or whatever the hell it is and finally I just scream: "Jesus Christ, Vanessa! Cut to the chase! Is Richard Harris a good fuck or not?!"

And Rule Number Two: No children. The only exception I ever made was for Tatum O'Neal after she was nominated for her Oscar. The Oscar nomination instantly makes you a Twinklie... I just don't get the appeal of "children." This one client squeezed out an infant and wanted to bring it by the house. I told her: "Why don't you drive past and let it wave?" ... Now Sigmund Freud – or better yet Monty Clift playing Sigmund Freud – would probably say my aversion to kids has something to do with my childhood.

She glances at the phone:

And since we appear to have some time, I'll tell you about that. Once upon a time I was born in Germany and...wait...for this I need fortification.

She looks around... Spots a little silver box on a table across the room... No way she's getting up.

Then she scans the audience. She selects a man.

You... Yes, you, honey. Come on up here. Sue needs you. Don't be shy. You're never going to make it in this town without some initiative. This is your big break, baby.

She finds an audience member to play along. Hereafter: The Unlucky Audience Member.

The Unlucky Audience Member heads to the stage.

Stop... Weren't you listening, honey? ... The carpet. Lose the shoes. Thanks.

She makes the Unlucky Audience Member take off his shoes.

No, we'll wait. It's not like we have anything else to do. Tick tick tick.

When his shoes are off…

Now could you be a sweetheart and get me that silver box?

The Unlucky Audience Member gets the silver box… Brings it to her.

Thanks, you're a doll. You may sit down again. Take the shoes. Don't be a stranger.

The Unlucky Audience Member gets his shoes and returns to his seat.

SUE opens the silver box. Removes a joint and lights it.

Ahhh.

I was born in Germany, a couple years ago. When I was eight Mr. Hitler started getting stroppy so my parents decided it was time to seek greener pastures. We packed up what we could carry and joined the ranks of sensible Jews who were getting gone. This was my father, my mother and me. … It was all pretty much like the Von Trapps in *The Sound of Music,* only without dreamy Christopher Plummer and all those not-up-to-their-usual-standards Rodgers and Hammerstein songs.

We settled in Utica, New York, where my playboy father quickly discovered there wasn't much of a market for émigré German playboys. He was a

feckless sort of man, honestly, but we had to eat, so
he ended up as a travelling salesman, which didn't
make him scream with joy.

I didn't speak a word of English so the first few
years were grim. I remember at school always
feeling outside looking in, you know? I would stand
there on the playground and watch the other kids
playing together, not twenty feet away. The most
popular girl was called Gladys Burton. She was
the ringleader, the star. I looked at her. What did
she have that I didn't? Why her and not me? …
Longest twenty feet there ever was… But I was too
embarrassed by my accent to talk to her, to even
make the effort. The fat little German Jewess? Come
on… I eventually learned English, almost entirely
through the movies. Lessoned by Joan Crawford
and Bette Davis and Joan Blondell in little fleapit
bijous across Utica, I picked it up. That's why I still
talk like a gum-cracking Warner Brothers second
lead. Once I had the rudiments of the language,
I knew I had to make the effort. Night before I
practiced saying it over and over: "Hello, my name
is Sue Mengers. Hello, my name is Sue Mengers.
No accent. No accent. Hello, my name is Sue
Mengers." Next day at recess I walked across the
playground… Maybe the bravest thing I ever did…
I go up to Gladys Burton.

"Hello, my name is Sue Mengers."

And she was nice. Thank God for that. My life
would probably have been entirely different if little
Gladys Burton had been a bitch.

So a couple years later my father kills himself. He
wasn't sick and he didn't leave a note. He killed
himself in a Time Square hotel room, which seems
redundant.

She takes a hit on the joint.

We never knew why. Well, living with my gorgon
of a mother might have had something to do with
it... But looking back I think it was this: his life
was never going to align with his self-image. He
was never going to be the soigné gentleman he
imagined. It wasn't going to be cigarette boats on
Lake Como; it was going to be third-class trains and
cold-water flats until the credits rolled. He died of
thwarted dreams, my dad... And you wonder why I
work so hard for my clients?

Well, my mother couldn't stand the shame his
suicide heaped on us in little old Utica so we bid
farewell to Gladys Burton and escaped to big old
New York City, where every third person is a fat
German Jewess and nobody gives a shit about
anything. We settled in the Bronx and it wasn't long
before my obsession with movies and movie stars
led me to the inevitable conclusion: I had to be an
actress! I had to! How could I not be part of those
ravishing fantasies that gave me the very language

I speak?! Why couldn't I be as sleek as Lauren Bacall? Why couldn't I crackwise like Rosalind Russell?

But to be a movie star I figured I should at least have a passing acquaintance with the art of acting... A notion a surprising number of our current movie stars seem hell-bent to disprove... So I signed up for a six week evening class at the Lizzie Borden School of Elocution and Rhetoric on 45th and Lex. First night of the class I get all dolled up in my cutest number, take twenty-seven trains in from the Bronx, and walk up the fabled stairs at 45th and Lex to seize my destiny... One look around... Holy shit! Everyone is prettier than me, even the boys. I felt like Judy Garland at the MGM School: on one side there's Elizabeth Taylor and on the other side there's Lana Turner. I mean. Fuck! ... There goes that dream.

She laughs.

But was your Sue deterred? No she was not. If the stage door was closed, there was always a window to jimmy open and scamper through. I started reading the trades looking for my window. In this life, kiddies, there's always a window. Ah ha! I answered an ad for a receptionist at the William Morris Talent Agency and scampered on through. As a secretary I answered the phones and I made coffee and I listened. I listened to every conversation I could, sometimes through the keyhole it must be said. I found out I loved it: I loved the business of the business. Why be a king when you can be a kingmaker?

She lights another cigarette. She's a two-fisted smoker: joint in one hand, cigarette in the other.

So there I was, a little pisher making 135 bucks a week, but I had a desk and a phone and damn if I wasn't going to get noticed. Flashing the William Morris name like an FBI badge, I went everywhere and met everyone. Night after night I was out pressing the flesh, charming my way, going to shows, going to dinners. Pretty soon people were asking about that cute little blond who seemed to know a lot of people and had opinions about which she was not shy. And she was kind of funny too, which was unusual in a city crammed with humorless Radcliffe dykes.

What was I doing? Crossing the playground. "Hello, my name is Sue Mengers, William Morris Agency."

You want to be a thing? Make yourself that thing.

We were all making ourselves up then. Not just me. Case in point: ... Now this may come as a shock to you but every single person who works in the theatre is gay. Without exception. So I was not unduly surprised when a client invited my boss and me out for a drink at a gay club. Frankly, it had been a long week and I didn't want to go. But your

Sue couldn't face the Bataan Death March back to
her Bronx walk-up without a canteen of sustenance,
so I went. Place was called The Lion... *(Glance to
the Unlucky Audience Member.)* ... You remember, the
place on 9th Street... There was a singer that night.
Her name was Barbara Streisand. Barb-a-ra. She still
had the other "a" then, that's how early this was...

> *SUE imagines the scene.*

She gets up there on this tiny stage with one little
spotlight, this funny-looking girl, all Second Hand
Rose, she shuffles around awkwardly, checks her
mike a few times, nervous chatter from her, people
are talking, no one gives a shit...

Then out of the corner of my eye I see her do
something I'll never forget. I'm sure no one else
noticed it. She makes the guy adjust the spotlight.
Like this forty watt spotlight with an amber gel in
the middle of this shitty gay bar. She makes him
move it until it's the way she wants... She took
the time to make a little magic. That's what a <u>star</u>
does... Now she's got my attention... And then she
sings.

> *Beat as she muses.*

After the show I marched up to her with all the
subtlety of a Panzer division rolling into Poland.
"Listen, kid, you're gonna go the distance. I can
see it. The rest of them, these fucking jamokes,

they can't. But I can. And I wanna be there... *(She smiles and extends her hand.)* ... Sue Mengers, William Morris Agency."

She looked at me. She took my hand.

Beat.

She picks up the phone... Listens for the dial tone.

CALL ME, YOU CUNT!

She places the phone down and continues amiably:

Anyway, back to me... The great day finally came when the big window opened. A young guy named Tom Korman with his own talent agency offered me my own desk. He took a chance I might make an agent. God Bless Tom Korman! Without Tom Korman, there's no Sue Mengers. Where would we be without those people who believe in us, those brave souls who take a second to glance our way and say, "What the fuck, why not?"

Korman and Associates – that's me, the associates – was a second-tier agency at best but goddamn it, I was an agent at last! I went to work doing what an agent does, which is essentially two things: signing and holding. You sign the talent and you hold on to them. In between – when time allows – you get them work. You talk them off the various ledges of show business. You make them happy. You make

them rich. You get them laid. You Sherpa up the
side of any mountain they choose. And along the
way – oh please god! – you have some laughs…
Now after all that time as a secretary I was straining
at the leash to start building my client list. I went
after everyone. Honey, I was so ambitious I would
have signed Martin Bormann. I signed Julie Harris
instead.

Add her to the list: Gladys Burton, Tom Korman,
and Julie Harris. She's a great actress and a great
friend. If you haven't seen her in *Member of the
Wedding* you have denied yourself one of the true
highlights of movie acting… My very first client.
My only client for a while… And she taught me a
lesson I've never forgotten: you have to speak to the
artists in their language, not yours. Julie talked to
me about Shakespeare and poetry, about drama of
substance, because that's what mattered to her. She
wasn't interested in box office receipts or boosting
her quotes. When I spoke with venality, her eyes
glazed over… After our first meeting I went to the
Public Library every day on my lunch hour and I
read Ibsen and Aristotle and Odets. The smile on
Julie's face the first time I quoted poetry. That smile
I'll treasure until my dying day.

Because here's the truth of agenting: you are the
public face of the client. You're representing them
literally and figuratively. A great agent is a great
chameleon: you have to become the client's mirror.
That's the reason clients leave mostly: they no

longer like the way the agent is presenting them to the world. Anyone with balls can make a cold call to David Merrick and bully and swear and play hardball. It takes a great deal more finesse to make those calls with sensitivity and nuance. When you call to get Julie Harris a job you don't say: "Listen, you motherfucker, give this bitch the part." You call, you make a sound like you're sipping tea; and you say "Good afternoon, Miss Julie Harris is considering a guest appearance on *Bonanza*, shall we discuss that?"

Then...the phone rings.

SUE jumps.

She lets it ring once...twice...a devilish glance to the audience...three times...

She finally answers, casually:

Tramont residence... Sissyyyy, hello! You're so sweet to call. You got a phone there on the farm I take it. That's a step in the right direction. How is every little thing? ... *(She mouths "Sissy Spacek" to the audience.)* ...uh-huh, uh-huh. Yeah, that's swell. Honey, we gotta talk about your representation. You know everything comes across my desk and I'm looking at the scripts out there and I'm sitting here worrying about you, I am, I'm fretful. There's a new Brian DePalma script nobody but me has seen that screams you and– ... *(Listens for a beat.)*

27

...uh-huh, uh-uh. Well let me tell you about it first
and then I'll sleep easily, totally selfish. Now don't
tell a soul but Brian's remaking *Scarface* with Al
Pacino and this could be a career-changing part for
you. Sissy Spacek in *Scarface*, what could be more
perfect!? ... *(Listens for a beat.)* ...uh-huh, uh-huh. I
know you just won the Oscar, but that was last year,
honey. What about next year? Don't you want two?
Listen, I'll send the script, you call, we talk, and
we're wearing Balenciaga at the Dorothy Chandler
this time next year! ... *(Laughs, listens for a beat.)*
...uh-huh, uh-huh. That's not all. I don't mean to
speak ill of any other agents but I gotta be honest
with you: I don't think your guys are thinking big
picture. By which I mean <u>recording</u>... *(She smiles,
she knows she's hit a nerve: gotcha.)* ... So I was talking
to David Geffen about how great you sounded in
Coal Miner's Daughter. "Why is this girl not under
contract, David? Why the hell isn't she cutting
albums left right and center? Now don't tell anyone
because the release doesn't go out until next week,
but David just signed Donna Summer for his label,
which is stratospheric, right? Why couldn't you
be next? Who couldn't build a label with Summer
and Spacek?! ... *(She listens for a beat.)* ... Well you
don't have to do what she does. You could do what
you do. That folk singing thing you do. I'll call
David tonight, honey. Point is that Sue loves you
and Sue's thinking about you and I would die for
the chance to represent you because– *(She listens
for a beat.)* ... uh-huh, uh-huh, uh-huh. What? Oh
my gosh! You just stop right there! I would never

try to poach a client from another agency! Never, ever! You should forgive that I'm concerned about your career and– *(She listens for a beat as she eats another chocolate.)* ...uh-huh, uh-huh... Listen, no one understands fidelity more than I do. I'm not saying that the fine gentlemen at CAA can't do their jobs, it's just that– *(She listens for a beat, getting more worked up now.)* ...uh-huh, uh-huh... Baby, you do what you want, Sue's always here, in your corner, life is long. But really, honey, isn't it time to shit or get off the pot? You're hot, I'm hot, town's hot, time's now, which I'm afraid your pseudo-Ivy-League-whiz-kid-boy-agents-slash-rentboys will fail to recognize. So you give it a good hard think, kid, and use your goddamn head. Smoke a joint, pluck a chicken, drive to the Piggly-Wiggly, whatever the fuck you do to relax, and consider what I am now saying to you: the most powerful talent agent in the entire fucking world is putting out her hand and you slap it away at the peril not to our friendship, which is unassailable, but to the peril of your immortal soul, or at least your immortal career, and singing career, and next Oscar, and Grammy, and everything I know will come your way, but only if you drop the Holly Hobbie bullshit and start acting like the strong, talented, decisive artist you are, or would want to be if any of those motherfuckers at CAA ever let you know you could be! Which you can! With me! Right now! Ciao, baby!

She hangs up.

She brushes back her hair, very ladylike again.

I've been trying to steal Sissy for years… In my
long pursuit of Miss Spacek I actually made
the pilgrimage to that farm she lives at. It's in a
mythical land called Virginia. So I get all dolled
up in my cutest little Chanel number and fly to
Middle Buttfuck where there's this guy waiting
for me in a jeep. Lemme tell you, Sue does not
do jeeps. General Patton does jeeps. But I'm on
a holy mission so I get in and endure the ride to
Sissy's "farm." I can only surmise it was a mud farm
because that's all there was. I get out. Sink three
inches. Chanel pumps stay behind as I tip-toe over
to meet Dame Spacek who's all dressed in early
Waltons. Then she proceeds to give me a tour of
the "farm" which only results in mud up to my
twat. Finally we retire to her house and have a cup
of tea, herbal, natch, and I proceed to tell her how
much her prick of an agent is ruining her career and
I hope she sees a future in mud farming because
that's where she's heading if she doesn't leave said
prick and sign with me. She's vague and moon-
beamy and promises to keep in touch. I get back
in the jeep, back to the airport, back to LA, leaving
a little trail of dried mud flakes snowing from my
twat.

Moral of the story: when you're trying to steal a
client, you do anything. So you lose a pair of savage
little Chanels; the commission on Sissy Spacek pays

for a whole boutique… The big picture, my friends.
The big picture.

You note I have no shame about saying I'm trying
to <u>steal</u> Sissy. We're all headhunters in my business.
It's a tough old game, Hollywood. Survival of the
fittest… Favorite book I never wrote: *I'll Eat You
Last: A Cannibal Love Story.*

She smiles and lights another joint, or cigarette, or both.

Now all these invaluable lessons about the
byzantine ways of the Movieland Empire I learned
when I finally made it out here to LA in 1968. By
now I'm working for Freddie Fields and David
Begelman at the company that became ICM, my
current home.

At first I was a little frog in a big pond so I had to
work at it. I had to get noticed.

Riding to the rescue on her white steed came
Barbra Streisand, who it should go without saying
has never been on a horse in her life, so I speak
figuratively. Barbra don't do livestock.

Here we were; two klutzy gals from the outer
boroughs amidst the lotus blossoms. The big
difference is that by then she was a major star and
I'm still low down in the credits. So Barbra started
schlepping me along to parties… "I'm gonna bring
my friend Sue… You mind if I bring my friend Sue

Mengers, you'll love her"… Being on Barbra's arm immediately gave me clout. Heads turned. People started to pay attention. There was a certain freak appeal for sure: women agents were almost unheard of. And a woman agent who drank and swore and knew what she was talking about and looked fucking adorable? Come on, I was made for this place!

What Barbra did was open the window for me. Once I was inside, it was up to me. So I went to work. I talked to everyone. I was persuasive, I was funny. Most of all, I was ferocious. To me "no" always meant "maybe."

Case in point: Gene Hackman.

Gene was an early client of mine, an early believer, and one of the best actors I know; incapable of being false on screen. We hear about this movie. It's perfect for him, the next rung up the ladder. It's the part of Popeye Doyle in *The French Connection.* I try to land it but Gene's never opened a movie as the lead, and he doesn't scream movie star handsome, so it's the definition of a <u>hard sell</u>… I go to work. I start calling. I'm on the phone five times a day to Billy Friedkin, the director. I'm on the phone hourly with Fox, the studio. They tell me "no." I hear "maybe." Meanwhile they're offering it to everyone in town. Paul Newman turns it down. Steve McQueen turns it down. Robert Mitchum turns it down. James Caan and Peter Boyle turn it down. I'm pitching for Gene like a motherfucker with every pass. Cha-ching: No sale.

Then one morning my spy at Fox tells me they're about to offer it to…wait for it…this is true… Jackie Gleason.

Well this is the last fucking straw, right? Now they're just slapping my tits! I stomp out of the house, get into my Bentley, light up a joint, and drive straight over to Billy Friedkin's house like a Valkyrie in heat. I pull up and park right in his driveway. I mean there's no way he can get out past me. I wait. He comes out to go to work.

"Billy, you're splitting my brain open over this goddamn picture! Is this a joke?! Jackie-fucking-Gleason?! What, was James Coco not available?!"

He says, "No, no, no, Sue, that's not right, we're not offering it to Gleason. We're about to make the offer to Charles Bronson."

This is a tactical error. He's told me something I don't know. This is the first I've heard of Charles Bronson. And fuck! This is bad. Bronson's a box office star and he'll take it…

I improvise but quick:

"Billy, Billy, Billy, think about this for five minutes. Popeye Doyle is a hulking Neanderthal of a character. You cast Charles Bronson and you've cast a hulking Neanderthal… Where's the irony? … You want a guy who looks like a brute, but inside the eyes you see feral intelligence. This is Gene Hackman! Smart as a whip, educated, former Marine, classical actor, did you see his Konstantine in *The Seagull* in New York? Fucking heart-stopping performance; broke your heart." … A part I have no idea if Gene Hackman ever played, by the way … "You cast Charles Bronson everyone says 'Look, there's Charles Bronson' and they stop believing in the story. It's just another Charles Bronson vehicle. But if you cast Gene Hackman you get someone the audience doesn't know, someone they'll believe, someone who just might not win: the underdog. You get that big, ugly potato face with the soul of a Beat poet. This is your Popeye Doyle!"

It's in his eyes. He's starting to see it. I take the shot:

"Listen, just hold the offer to Bronson five minutes and meet Gene, see if I'm not right. One measly sit down is all I ask. Call it a favor to me. You don't click, fine, you make the offer to Bronson and everyone's happy, most of all me. Whattaya think?"

He says, "Come on, Sue, would you move your car?"

"Not until you tell me you'll meet with Gene."

I light a cigarette. A very long cigarette.

He sighs. "Favor to you. That's all."

I say, "Baby, you're the best."

Year later Gene and Billy pick up their Oscars...
That's how you do the job, kids.

She smiles, loves a happy ending.

*She picks up another chocolate... Puts it down...
Immediately picks it up again and eats it.*

Pretty soon you can see how I was getting the
reputation of an agent who fought for my clients;
who wasn't afraid to take on the big boys. The
trickle of clients became a flood. After Gene came
Candy Bergen, Mike Nichols, Michael Caine,
George Segal, Herbert Ross, Anthony Newley,
Dyan Cannon, Bob Fosse, Sidney Lumet, Burt
Reynolds, Cybill Shepherd, Ryan O'Neal, Rod
Steiger, Peter Bogdanovich, Gore Vidal, on and on.

*She puts her feet up on the coffee table, sinking deeper
into the sofa.*

So in the blink of the proverbial eye, I'm living the
life I always dreamed about... I'm Bette Davis. I'm
Ava Gardner. Sometimes I'm Broderick Crawford,
but still... Point is: I'm not just Barbra's friend, I'm
Sue Mengers. People took my calls instantly: the
only real measure of success in Hollywood by the
way.

I'm the toast of the town. Clients are getting rich. I start getting press. Mike Wallace does a piece on me in *60 Minutes.* I'm not just representing stars; I <u>am</u> a star... Cue the ominous organ music.

But before all that, let me share with you the Five Golden Rules of being a great agent.

She realizes her glass is empty...glances over at the sideboard across the room loaded with liquor... No way she's getting up.

She looks again to the Unlucky Audience Member, in her baby voice:

Honey, Sue's thirsty.

She shakes her empty glass.

Come on, baby, you're on again.

She makes the Unlucky Audience Member return to the stage.

If he doesn't remember about his shoes, she reminds him to take them off:

Shoes... Now go over there and bring me the Lalique decanter. Go on, chop-chop.

He goes to the sideboard. It's filled with different decanters.

She purrs:

It's the tall one, dear.

The Unlucky Audience Member brings her the tall decanter.

I'd ask you to join me, but that might encourage an unhealthy familiarity. Thanks, you're a peach, truly; now get the fuck out of here.

The Unlucky Audience Member starts to go…

Wait, wait… Honey, come back here…

The Unlucky Audience Member returns…

Have a chocolate, sweetie.

She gives him a chocolate from the dish on the coffee table.

You enjoy that now. Bye bye.

As the Unlucky Audience Member gets his shoes and returns to his seat she considers him, shaking her head:

Sometimes I don't think God sent his smartest Jews to Hollywood.

SUE pours herself a fresh drink… Sips… Ahh.

So you want to be a Superagent? All you have to do is follow Sue's Five Golden Rules. The more enterprising of you will want to take notes.

Rule Number One: Never Blow a Deal on Money.

In Hollywood, money doesn't really mean anything, it's just a way to keep score... It's kind of like the Easter Bunny: nobody needs it, but it's nice when it hops into your lap and warms your cooze... Let's face it, most movie stars have more money than they could spend in a hundred lifetimes, so five or ten or fifty grand here or there doesn't really matter. What <u>does</u> matter is building a career and making the smart choices. When you're an agent you have to be a giraffe: you stand looking over the trees, checking out the predators lying in wait, and hopefully see a way to the next watering hole... And a <u>smart</u> agent knows when to take less money for a job that moves your client closer to the watering hole. Big picture, remember?

Robert Evans and Roman Polanski are casting *Chinatown*. For the female star opposite Jack Nicholson they're waffling between Jane Fonda and my client, Faye Dunaway. It's coming down to the wire. My spies at Paramount tell me they're getting ready to offer it to Fonda. I go into Great White mode. I call up Bobby Evans, who I know forever:

"Bobbeeeee, listen, this movie's going to be hard enough to make without having to deal with Jane's mishegoss, you know what I mean? You have to tell her to fuck off, honey, because you're going to lose Dunaway if you don't. Now I shouldn't be telling you this, but Arthur Penn wants Faye for his new picture, so I need an answer by close of business tomorrow or we're taking it, shitting you I am not. And we won't take a penny less than 250,000, you hear me, you prick! 250,000!"

Slam down the phone. Bobby calls an hour later:

"Mengella, I hear Faye's hard to work with."
"What?! Compared to Hanoi Jane and her legions of protesting vets? Come on! And we want 250,000, you fucker!"
"75,000 or I'm calling Jane."
"Fuck you. We're taking the Arthur Penn movie!"
"Fuck you. We're casting Jane."
Slam! Slam!

I spend an hour pretending to think about it; then I call Bobby:

"Honnneeeeeey, I spoke to Faye. She's crazy hot to work with Jack, so we'll take the measly 75,000. We got a deal?"
"We got a deal."
"And guess what? There was no Arthur Penn movie! I made it up! HA!"
"Guess what? Fonda turned us down yesterday. HA!"

She laughs.

God! I love the game! ... So in this case, getting
Faye Dunaway that part to move her career forward
was worth more than the money. Looking back on
her career you can see it clearly: no *Chinatown* no
Network no Oscar. The trick is seeing it <u>before</u> it
happens: all the way to the watering hole, baby.

And by the way, Faye never liked me and I never
liked her. She stayed with me five minutes. Wins the
Oscar and then she's out: bye-bye Sue... I do dryly
note with a certain amount of schadenfreude that
her last paying job was portraying Miss Eva Peron
in a TV movie. Who's laughing now, bitch?

So: Never Blow a Deal on Money.

Rule Number Two: Never Remind Them.

Here's another reason so many clients dump an
agent once they get successful: because you remind
them of when they were hungry. When they're on
the way up, they'll do anything for you. But once
they get a taste of success, as night follows day, they
start to hate you specifically because they used to
need you.

So for fuck's sake don't compound the problem
by reminding them of the "good old days" when
you were all young and eager and up-and-coming.
Movie stars have already up-and-come; they have

came-and-are. That's why they're movie stars.
There's nothing more present tense then a movie
star. You only talk to them about the future, never
the past. And if you're representing Miss Diana
Ross – as I did – you might want to avoid saying the
following as you walk the red carpet at the Oscars
with her: "Wow, Diana, long way from the days of
blowing Berry Gordy in the back of the limo, huh?"

She laughs.

So: Never Remind Them.

Rule Number Three: Never Tell Them the Truth.

Clients always say: "Come on, Sue, give it to me
straight, don't sugar coat it." Jesus God, not a one of
them could survive a single phone call that wasn't
coated with enough sugar to make Tony the Tiger
puke! You think any of them really want to know
SOYLENT GREEN IS PEOPLE?!

No, they do not… You never tell clients the whole
truth. You tell them just enough of the truth,
carefully shaded to make them feel as young and
successful and rich as possible at all times.

So, yes, I see you sitting there very righteously
saying: "But surely, Sue, you owe them the truth."
… Okay. Try looking into the eyes of someone
you love and saying this… "You're too old. You're
not hot anymore. They want the younger version

of you. They want the thinner version of you...
No, darling, they want you for the part of the
sister...for the best friend...for the sidekick...for
the grandmother... Maybe it's time to think about
TV? Maybe it's time to think about dinner theatre?
Maybe it's time to think about retirement? ... You
do not exist."

Careful... The skin of dreams is so thin. You
poke one little hole and all the air hisses out. All
movie people really have, most of them, is their
confidence. You take that away and...

> *She shakes her head.*

> *Beat.*

Julie Harris. You know how much I love this lady...
Recently she's not so hot. Time happens, right? *East
of Eden* is a long time ago. "Who's Julie Harris?" ...
But she's desperate to play Mary Todd Lincoln in
this TV thing. I go to the mat. I try everything. I
drive over there. I talk to the network. I talk to the
director. I offer bribes. I offer deals. I go flat out.
No good... "Too old. Not sexy enough." Like that
famous sex-kitten Mary Todd Lincoln, right?! ... So
I have to tell Julie. We have lunch so I can do it in
person... I'm dreading it... I tell her the director has
a hard-on for whoever they cast; nothing personal,
nothing to do with her.

She looks at me. She knows.

The smart ones always know.

Beat.

So: Never Tell Them the Truth.

Rule Number Four: Never Lie to Them.

Self-explanatory.

And Rule Number Five, the final rule: Know the Spouse.

Which brings us, invariably, to Ali MacGraw.

Ali was my favorite client ever. She's a goddess; like from another universe, she floats through ours, touching lives, making the world a more graceful place. I love her to little tiny pieces... I signed her right after she married Bobby Evans. She hits it big in *Love Story*. She gets the Oscar nomination and I get her on the cover of *Time*. She's respectful and funny and – oy – so beautiful. Ali and Bob are burning up the red carpet like nothing since Gable and Lombard. She's happy, I'm happy. What could possibly go wrong?

I'll tell you in two words... Four words... That cunt Steve McQueen.

So I'm busy playing giraffe, taking care of Ali. Maybe she's getting typecast in all these preppy parts? Maybe we should look for something different? She likes the idea of challenging herself with something new. This offer comes in: *The Getaway*. Sam Peckinpah directing. Ali opposite Steve McQueen. We grab it. They make it. She falls in love. She divorces Bobby Evans. She marries McQueen.

Nooooow... I know you're not supposed to speak ill of the dead...

She looks at the audience wickedly.

Carefully fires up a joint... Ahh.

Settles in.

Steve McQueen was a total fake. This cult of personality that's grown up around him since his death is crap. He was an abusive, alcoholic, misogynistic, loutish, pretentious, mean, mean, manic depressive. That motherfucker ruined Ali's career! He was so fucking insecure! He couldn't stand her star wattage, so he pushed her into the shadows. He makes her move into this isolated house out in Malibu and she becomes his "old lady" who's expected to have dinner on the table every night at six for Steve and his stuntmen buddies. And she did! And she did! This is Ali-fucking-MacGraw, barefoot and pregnant, waiting on that cocksucker hand and foot!

She's getting angrier in the retelling:

Of course she should have told him to fuck off!
Of course she should have fought for her career!
Everyone told her. Me loudest of all: "Why the fuck
are you letting this man take away your livelihood
and your dignity?! This is your moment, Ali, it
might never come again! You gotta be smart!"

You will not be surprised to hear that Steve loathed
me. Hated it when I called, knew I was trying to
get Ali back to work. He grunted something and
then handed the phone to her without a word,
when he didn't just hang up. Had all the manners of
Richard Speck... Early on she used to bring him to
my dinner parties. He got so nervous about being
in a room full of smart, tall people that he would
have to get stoned beforehand. Then he would just
stand in the corner, trying to look deeply brooding.
But he was a fake about that too. He didn't really
brood. He'd just scrunched up his face and try to
look deep; ended up looking like Kermit the Frog
thinking about Auschwitz.

But she loved him. This was her choice... This
was her heart. And it lied to her... You saw it
happening. It killed you.

Beat.

Or maybe this is what love looks like. Maybe it was
right for her, but wrong for me. What the hell do I

know? When the clapping stops, I'm not exactly an expert on much of anything.

Beat.

So day comes I have to have it out with Ali. She's choosing not to work and the offers are drying up. If she's going to salvage her career she's got to get back to work. Rest of your life, baby, you in or out?

I drive out to Malibu... I'm nervous... I adore this girl. I'm readying every argument in my head. I'm going to have to give her both barrels, which is what you do for people you love; you give it to them stone cold. She can take it...

She slows, remembering the moment...

I pull up... She walks out of the house to meet me. Her son Josh is on her hip...

She smiles... She's <u>radiant</u>... I look at her...

"Are you happy, Ali?"

"Yeah, Sue, I am."

I give her a kiss. I turn right around and drive away. I try not to look back.

Beat.

Final Rule: Know the Spouse.

Beat.

She takes off her glasses, rubs her eyes.

She puts the glasses back on, like armor.

Not that I had all that much time to worry about
Ali, because I'm in the Barbra Streisand business.
When you're in the Barbra Streisand business
it ain't part time, and there are no weekends or
holidays... Here's what most people don't get about
Barbra: she's wicked smart. She's also what they call
a "perfectionist." There's no detail too small. She
walks in here right now she'll have rearranged the
pillows and moved all the furniture in ten minutes,
or she'd have you do it. The whole world's her
stage and she's constantly adjusting the spotlight,
you know what I mean? ... It's not for vanity; it's
for artistry. ... She's got that rarest of things in
performers: she's got taste.

About everything but which parts to play... Jesus
Christ, I battered my poor head black and blue
against the wall trying to make her take the right
roles. I argue, I beg, I cajole, I threaten, I weep.
She won't be rushed. She won't be manipulated.
She knows her worth... So she turns down *Cabaret.*
So she turns down *The Exorcist.* So she turns down
Klute. What does she want to play? A girl who
dressed like a boy so she can study Talmudic law for

fuck's sake! She drives you crazy. But still you love
her. You should hate her, but you love her. I don't
know how she does it.

Sometimes your job is just to make her laugh. Or
calm her the fuck down.

Back in '69 when Charlie Manson and his family
were getting particularly madcap with the cutlery,
she goes bananas. She's absolutely sure she's next
on the hit list. She calls me in a panic:

"Sue. I know I'm next. These people hate Jews.
They'll kill anyone. What should I do? Should I
move? Should I get a gun? Should I hide? Should I
convert? Oh mighty God I know I'm next!"

I said, "Don't worry, honey, they're not killing stars,
only featured players."

She laughs.

She glances at the phone.

I'm sure she went to those motherfuckers at CAA.

For you civilians out there, CAA is Creative Artists
Agency, the fastest rising of the so-called New Wave
agencies; the shape of things to come we are all
breathlessly promised. They've built the agency
on a puritanical screed of complete dedication:
an Armani-clad samurai culture of monkish

sublimation of the individual to the corporate entity, to quote their mentor, Stalin... Oh did I say Stalin? I meant Mike Ovitz.

No, Mike's a good boy. The kind of guy you'd loooove to get stuck on a lifeboat with. Never forget the first time I sat with Mike. He's getting all hot talking about "turnaround negative cost pickups" and "merchandizing synergy against backend residual options on a sliding scale of first dollar gross." It's like some language I don't speak he's making up as he goes... He's honestly more interested in who's making what than who's screwing who. One of us is in the wrong town... Finally I interrupt the accounting lesson to say, "But, Mike, honey, do you actually like movies?" ... This makes him blink... I ask him, "What's your favorite movie?" ... I can see the wheels spinning. Literally inside his forehead I can see the little bumps as the gears turn. He's trying to give me the answer he thinks I want; the answer that won't lose him any status, nothing too commercial or he'll seem frivolous, nothing too arty or he'll seem pretentious. He finally narrows his eyes to cold little slits and says... "*Bambi*."

She laughs.

I lose about a client a month to CAA. So does everyone... I've seen the future. And, kids, it's not a lot of laughs.

Beat.

But, hell, I figure if I can survive both Adolph Hitler and *All Night Long* I can survive anything... *All Night Long*...the movie... You know, my <u>husband's</u> movie? ... Of course you've all seen it?

She gazes sternly over the audience for a beat.

All the trouble with Barbra really began with the infamous *All Night Long*. So Jean-Claude's trying to set it up for himself to direct. It's about a depressed middle-aged guy working the nightshift in a drugstore in the Valley who falls in love with a local gal. It's the kind of quirky little character movie they don't make anymore. Nary a superhero or light saber in sight. About which I can only say this: what the fuck's an Ewok?! I mean those smashed-in faces that look like gaping twats? Come on!

Anyway, this movie ain't *Star Wars* and Universal ain't gonna make it without some kind of name attached, so I start working on Gene Hackman. Gene does depressed middle-age better than anyone, right? And he owes me from *The French Connection*. Gene's a mensch and signs on to play the lead. Universal is over the moon they got Hackman in this runt of a picture. They cast Lisa Eichhorn as the gal. They start shooting. They stop shooting. It's not going well. Turns out, surprise, surprise, Lisa Eichhorn is no Glenda Jackson. Rushes are dire.

Studio's unhappy. Miss Eichhorn has to go. Gene's miserable. Jean-Claude's desolate. Sue goes to work.

I call Barbra and tell her I have a movie for her. She's in the middle of writing her cross-dressing Jew movie, so she could use a break. She says yes.

Now, in retrospect, this wasn't the wisest call I ever made. Is it just possible audiences won't want to see La Streisand playing a bored Valley hausfrau in this oddball movie? This question I did not ask myself. Que sera sera.

I start negotiating for Barbra and I play tough with Universal. She's white hot coming off *The Main Event* and her album "Guilty" is top of the charts. The studio knows this could be a magic moment, so they bite the big bullet. Biggest bullet there ever was. I get Barbra 4.5 million and 15% of the gross for 27 days of work. It's the most an actress has ever been paid. The town is stunned. They make the movie. *Gone With the Wind* it is not. It cost around 10 mill, ends up taking in 4, which, wags point out, is less than Barbra's salary... Look, movies fail all the time, it happens every day. But this was a public humiliation for Barbra Streisand. And for me.

You feel the backlash like a Malibu wildfire. Whispers that roar. "Sue Mengers forced her clients into her husband's movie." "She betrayed Streisand." "She lost Hackman." "The arrogance." "Serves her right." ... Before long the whispers turn into headlines. They see blood in the water. Suddenly I'm vulnerable.

And they all wait gleefully for the giant to fall.

So maybe I was off my game. Maybe I was overconfident. Maybe I forgot my own rules. Who the fuck knows? ... Maybe when I crossed the playground and said "Hello, my name is Sue Mengers" Gladys Burton looked back and said "Used to be."

So big deal. Clients leave. They've been leaving for a while actually. Peter Bogdanovich goes. Candy Bergen goes. Burt Reynolds goes. Cybill Shepherd goes. Sidney Lumet goes. Michael Caine goes. Gene Hackman goes... Ali goes... Julie Harris goes... Barbra...

Beat.

Hey, it's part of the job. I'm signing new clients all the time. And we'll all be–

The phone rings.

SUE jumps.

She answers almost immediately:

Tramont residence... Oh, Richard, hello! Honey, I'm just on the edge of my seat to see you tonight –

figuratively speaking because I'm actually ass-deep on the sofa just a teeny-weeny bit high... *(She listens for a beat.)* ...uh-huh...oh... *(She's surprised at what she's hearing.)* ... Hey, don't give it a second thought. We'll miss you, honey. You rest up and we'll see you next time. Bye bye, love.

She hangs up.

Beat.

Her hand rests on the phone for a moment.

Richard Dreyfuss cancelled for tonight. Richard Dreyfuss. Cancelled.

Beat.

The implications of this are profound to her.

She lights another joint or cigarette.

You ever seen that movie *The Poseidon Adventure?* I have. Goddamn that's fine entertainment. And I took particular relish in seeing so many former clients being drowned. I don't want to spoil it for you but the conclusion is very uplifting... Only the B-stars survive... Just like life.

Beat.

I'll tell you, in my more lucid moments I think about getting out of the game. Leave showbiz, split this town. Give up the dinners, the parties, the openings; the whole magilla.

I think when I retire I'll take a trip to Israel. Maybe I'll go with Barbra and she can out-Jew everyone. That would be fun. We would laugh... I guess that's what's changed about Hollywood most. We used to laugh more. Honey, we used to have fun.

But the New Hollywood is upon us. Yeah, partly it's a matter of style. These new agents aren't assaulting Billy Friedkin in his driveway. They're polite, subtle men who don't work on intimidation and aggression. They don't shout, they purr. They don't attack, they finesse. They're not angry... With me you get all the crayons in the box, even the ugly ones, even the angry ones. But never boring.

Trust me; you'll miss me when I'm gone.

Beat.

She glances at the phone ruefully. Shakes her head.

Typical.

She checks her watch.

Okay, kiddies, this has been a joy, I'm faint from the sheer ecstasy. But now Sue has to get ready

for the big party with all my lovely Twinklies.
Yes, believe it or not, I must be made even <u>more</u>
beautiful. My squadron of stylists, primpers and
morticians will arrive shortly. Don't bump into them
on your way out.

She braces herself and then...

<u>*She stands.*</u>

Ta-da.

She looks over the audience.

Of course I would ask you to stay but...well...look
at you.

She nods to the Unlucky Audience Member:

You've got some potential, honey. Keep at it,
nowhere to go but up. Maybe TV.

*She slowly jiggles toward the exit. It's a major production
number.*

She stops at the doorway out.

Turns back to the audience.

One last tip from Sue... Go ahead, cross the
playground. What have you got to lose? After all,
the credits roll sooner than you think.

She's about to exit when...

The phone rings.

She looks at it... A thousand miles away by the sofa.

She glances to the audience. Hell no.

She laughs.

Now get the fuck out of my house.

She exits as "Stoney End" by Barbra Streisand is heard.

And the curtain falls on the wonderful world of Sue Mengers. Here and then gone. Never to come again.

The End.

BY THE SAME AUTHOR

RED

9781840029444

Under the watchful gaze of his young assistant and the threatening presence of a new generation of artists, Mark Rothko takes on his greatest challenge yet: to create a definitive work for an extraordinary setting.

A moving and compelling account of one of the greatest artists of the 20th century whose struggle to accept his growing riches and praise became his ultimate undoing.

Nominated for 7 Olivier Awards (2009) and
Winner of 6 Tony Awards (2010) including Best New Play.

'A fresh, exciting portrait of a brilliant mind.'
Ben Brantley, *The New York Times*

'Smart and scintillating. *RED* deftly conjures what most plays about artists don't: The exhilaration of the act.'
John Lahr, *The New Yorker*

PETER AND ALICE

9781849434744

When Alice Liddell Hargreaves met Peter Llewelyn Davies at the opening of a Lewis Carroll exhibition in 1932, the original Alice in Wonderland came face to face with the original Peter Pan. In John Logan's remarkable new play, enchantment and reality collide as this brief encounter lays bare the lives of these two extraordinary characters. This is the new play from Academy Award-winning screenwriter and playwright John Logan.

'Shattering in its intensity...the distressful, healing empathy which great theatre produces.' Libby Purves, *The Times*

'Bold, daring theatre that is unquestionably touched by greatness.' Christopher Hart, *Sunday Times*

'poetic and achingly wistful... Logan's writing is filled with arresting images...rather beautiful.' Sam Marlowe, *Arts Desk*

WWW.OBERONBOOKS.COM

Follow us on www.twitter.com/@oberonbooks
& www.facebook.com/oberonbook